I0149201

All Scripture references taken from the KJV of the Holy Bible.

## SUNBLOCK: Triangular Powers

Dr. Marlene Miles

Freshwater Press, USA

ISBN: 978-1-960150-39-4

Paperback Version

Copyright 2023 by Dr. Marlene Miles

All rights reserved.

# Table of Contents

# SUNBLOCK

## *Triangular Powers*

Freshwater

For every evil under the sun,

There is a remedy,

Or there is none,

If there be one, try and find it.

If there be none, never mind it.

**Mother Goose**

# Under the Sun

Every evil under the sun--, you know there will be evils under the sun because we are in the flesh. There will be harmful things, hurtful things, sad things, painful things in life. They come to us because life comes to us, and we encounter *stuff*.

There is a remedy for what happens under the sun.

Let's talk first about the sun. The sun does have great purposes in our life. We need the sun to live. Sunlight kills bacteria. Not all of it, but it kills a lot of it. People tend to get more respiratory infections in the wintertime, because there's less sunlight, so there's more bacteria in the air, and on surfaces. People are indoors more, in enclosed spaces and they are touching things--, ick, *ewww*!

To benefit us, sunlight can reduce blood pressure, makes us happy, right? It can reduce the risk of cancer. On the other hand, too much sunlight can *cause* cancer.

The sun can strengthen our bones by helping our bodies make Vitamin D. The sun can improve our sleep quality. Hey, we're outside, we're hanging out, we're active and getting tired. Of course, we will sleep well at night if we get good and tired during the day.

But too much sunlight--, too much of any good thing or the wrong use of a good thing can cause harm and pain. It can cause negative things to happen to us.

Too much sunlight causes sunburn, sun rashes, skin diseases, skin disorders, Melanoma, and related ills.

This is why we use sunblock to protect us from the negative effects of something good that could be misused or overused. It's why we need sunblock. It's why this book is called Sun Block.

We need to block the harmful effects of the sun against us and against our lives. In Book 1 of the *Triangular Powers* Series, POWERS ABOVE we began talking about heavenly powers. We talked about the *Powers Above*. This book, **SUN BLOCK** will be about the sun. Book 3 of the Series is entitled, **Don't Swear by the Moon**, and Book 4 is entitled, **Star Struck**.

The misuse, abuse or incorrect use of anything can be harmful as well. The sun can be abused and used in ways that are harmful to mankind. For this reason, we will need a *spiritual* sunblock to keep us spiritually protected and safe.

This book will explain so much more.

# The Sun

The sun is one of the *Triangular Powers*, it is one of the celestial *Powers Above*, and it is something that the enemy has found a way to use *against* mankind. But God did not intend for the sun to hurt us.

Recall, we differentiate the Powers Above as the celestial powers and then there are the powers spoken of in Ephesians 6; those are the fallen angels and Satan himself. As evil goes, they are the ones using the Triangular Powers against mankind.

For we wrestle not against flesh and blood, but against principalities, against powers, against the rulers of the

darkness of this world, against spiritual wickedness in high *places.*
(Ephesians 6:12)

God made the entire universe. He made all the elements and the heavens. He made the *Powers Above* in the heavens and the *powers below.* God, Himself lives in the 3rd Heaven. He is the mightiest of **Powers Above** and all powers. Power belongs to God.

Then, there's a second heaven. We talked about this extensively in **POWERS ABOVE: Triangular Powers**, please review it if you need to. Satan has set up shop in the 2nd heaven. Of course, Satan is always trying to be like God, so why wouldn't he try that?

Satan is in the 2nd heaven, confirming that there *is* spiritual wickedness in high places as Ephesians 6:12 states.

Here, high places refers to heavenly places, not the *high places* where people, in the natural, in the Old Testament, set up altars necessarily. The Old Testament high places were in hills and mountains and those altars were set up to deploy, in an evil way, the *powers* in the high places in the heavenlies. This they did (and do) in attempts to bring some of that force or effect into Earth to accomplish their own personal desires, and that usually is against mankind.

The powers in the heavens are the *evil spirits* that the Lord Jesus will shake from the heavens when He comes back to Earth in power and glory.

In the second heavens there are principalities, powers, rulers of wickedness and darkness in those high places. Those powers are fallen angels. That's who is warring against us, and that's who our war is against.

God, in Genesis created the heavens, the heavenly powers, the sun, the moon, the stars to rule over the day, to rule over the night and to give us light in the nighttime. They are powerful lights that govern the Earth, and those lights **affect** us.

The sun rules the day, the moon rules the night and then there are the stars as well. Man has been set in authority here on Earth, and in Dominion. We have command over all the works of God's hands and over these celestial bodies, the sun, the moon, stars, and we have command in the Earth.

# Take Command

We have authority, and we're set in Dominion. So, when we speak, things should <u>happen</u>. That is, *if* we speak. We need to speak. If we don't speak the Word of God; if we don't speak what God says, evil entities and evil human agents will speak, and they'll use God's creation *against us* because they hate us.

For this reason (and others) we need to command the day, command the morning, command the night as we *speak*. Sadly, the heart of man is wicked, it's evil, especially in a jealous-hearted person. Jealousy and other works of the flesh go all the way back to Cain and Abel. Since then, man has devised a way to use the power in the sun *against* other men in the Earth. Evil agents have realized the powers of the sun, moon, and stars and have devised or have been taught to misuse them in a negative but powerful way. We need to know how to handle ourselves and how to be victorious when coming under attack from these evil, human agents.

This could be why even though you feel like you're walking upright before the Lord, you're fasting, you're praying, you're paying tithes and giving offerings--, you are doing everything you're supposed to be doing in the faith, but your prayers, your deliverance, or your answers to prayers are delayed or hindered. Evil human agents abusing these heavenly powers is why your life may be affected in a negative way by their activities. Especially life those activities are unchecked. The reason could be that evil human agents are using *Triangular Powers* against you, so you need to know what to do. You're walking upright, but you may be wondering where are the things that apply to your life? To your peace? Where are the things that God has promised you? Where are the things that you know you should have, but don't? Who or what is blocking your life and your good things?

# Sun Worship

**We do not worship the sun, we do not worship the moon. We do not worship stars. We do not worship angels**. We do not worship the Earth.

People who lay around outside, getting sun tans, are called sun worshippers. That just means they like to go outside. I'm talking about people who actually worship the sun as a deity—we don't do that. We only worship the Only Living God.

In ancient Egypt, the 14th century before Christ, there was a pagan religion called *Atenism*. Those people worshipped the sun. Other cultures and religions have also practiced sun worship.

We don't do that.

The Incas in Peru, the Nabataeans who built the city of Petra in Jordan worship the sun, and Shintoism is a practice of sun worship in Japan. One of the most popular *little g gods in* the Incan, civilization in South America was considered to be a sun *god.*

We do not worship the sun. The sun is not a God. There is no "god" that we worship or serve in the sun. The Only Living God does not live in the sun.

If anything lives in the sun, based on some things I've read, it could be some of the fallen angels, and you have to know that anything that could live in the sun or survive in the sun, or even in the depths of the water, or any uninhabitable places has to be pretty sturdy. And you will need some serious, spiritual weapons to defeat them. You won't beat them with a bow and arrow or shoot them with an AK or something. That won't work. You can't defeat something spiritual with a natural weapon.

So, when we talk about defending ourselves against spiritual wickedness in high places, we're talking about spiritual entities. Therefore, we need spiritual weapons.

We need to build up our spiritual weapons and our spiritual armory. Taking care of your body is important in your life, but building up your flesh is of little value against *spiritual* enemies. We need God, we need the Holy Spirit. We need the Armory and the power of God to be victorious over the spiritual weapons of spiritual wickedness.

So, the sun is in the sky doing what it's supposed to be doing according to what God planned. It gives us light, it gives us energy, warmth, kills bacteria, helps us to make Vitamin D. But, to the negative, the sun can smite, it can burn.

The sun shall not smite thee by day, nor the moon by night. (Psalm 121:6)

The sun can rule not just over the day but over all mankind. If the sun refuses to shine, we'll be cold; we might freeze. We'll be living in darkness. We wouldn't have any food. There be no photosynthesis, there would be no animals for food.

The sun can affect all of the nations, all of the Earth. The sun is powerful and when abused, the *Triangular Powers* can cause sickness, disease, disaster, death.

Occultic evil tries to harness the power of the sun to block destinies, to block marriages, because out of marriages come godly seeds. The devil is ever trying to block that. The devil and his evil human agents try to block wealth from people and divert it to themselves or others who have contracted their evil services.

The light of the sun can be programmed by evil to bring disaster, calamity, mishaps. They can project poverty and the loss of wealth against people that they want to destroy. They can project backwardness into people's lives by using the sun.

Are you prayed up? Stay prayed up.

# It Can't Be This Difficult

**Have you've ever noticed that quirky, really weird things happen to you that don't happen to everybody else?** Easy things that are easy for everybody else is hard to near impossible, or actually impossible for you. Why? Why are you having failure when most people don't have failure at a thing? *Triangular Powers.*

When those powers abused, when certain types of evil people are using *Triangular Powers*, especially the sun, and if unopposed they can really jack up a person's life.

They usually and especially enjoy trying to pull pastors into sin and backsliding, especially the popular pastors, the ones in the public eye. They do that to disgrace them.

In October, witches fast, they proclaim an evil fast other times of the year as well, but October is a favorite month. It's their highest evil, HOLLOWDAY month (*my word*). A lot of them fast all of October, with the goal to pull down and destroy pastors. Because if they smite the shepherd then the whole congregation will scatter.

If pastors had any idea about that well-dressed, charismatic someone that just came into their church on any given Sunday--, that they are on *assignment* and who they're on assignment for, a lot of pastors wouldn't behave the way that they do and get caught in terrible situations.

There are many people who are on evil assignments, even in church, especially in the Church.

They are demonic agents and there are many other people who are being *used* by the devil, but don't even realize that they are also demonic agents. The pastor's fall is usually from a carnal sin or money. But most often, it's carnal sin.

Let me ask you, if some witches and wizards can take a pastor down or out, does that mean that pastor was or was not prayed up? And if that pastor wasn't prayed up, then do you think he's praying for *you* and not *himself*? You need to be sure you are prayed up, yourself. See to it yourself. Of course, pastors, intercessors, and deliverance workers can take some hits and be attacked spiritually for praying for others. So, you should pray for your spiritual leaders and anyone else who prays for you. Be sure to pray for yourself because if you don't the attack will come to the person who is praying for you. When you don't take responsibility to pray, it's a though you are directing the demons over to the pastor's house so he can get you out of the spiritual trouble you got yourself into. Is that fair?

# Atheists

So-called **people** are using the *Triangular Powers,* to keep seekers and God's people away from God, to keep people living a random life with no purpose. As devil agents, they desire that people have a wandering, unstable, nomadic life. Those who abuse the *Triangular Powers* are the people that are against God.

Did you know that there are 500 million atheists and agnostics in the world? 500 million people *dissing* God.

The *Triangular Powers* are working for evil to deafen the ears of mankind to the Gospel of Jesus Christ. *Triangular Powers* are used to set up barriers against the breakthroughs in the lives of an unbeliever, a seeker, and the believer.

More than a million Americans identify as pagans or witches. Worldwide, Atheists make up about 3% of the population. There are 500 million atheists and China has the number one number of atheists. These are people who just can't be bothered to think that there's anything greater than themselves.

Don't get me wrong, I know some of these people. Everyone I know is not a Christian. And there are still some people who pretend to be Christians, and there are some who *think* they are Christians because their grandmother was saved. But until you accept the Lord Jesus Christ yourself as your own Lord and Savior, you're not saved.

When you do this, you also have to renounce all other sins and practices, including witchcraft, divination, tarot, crystals, horoscopes, astrology, numerology, Angel numbers, acupuncture, tattoos, craniosacral manipulation, Reiki healing, and all other kinds of "energy healing" and other "energy manipulation."

You can't just mix all that stuff together. God's not hearing you. God's not. You're not a Christian until you've given up that stuff.

Read your Bible and it'll clearly tell you what Christians do and what they practice, as well as what they don't do.

# Believers

So you are a believer, who has been believing God, you've been fasting and praying and following the rules, studying your Bible. Where's your breakthrough? You need to suspect *Triangular Powers*— suspect people using the power of **Triangular Powers** against your successes and breakthroughs.

If you haven't commanded the day, commanded the night, commanded these *Triangular Powers* to **not** work against you and instead to work in your favor you may be stagnated in life. We're gonna pray , but if you haven't done it, that could be why you don't have a breakthrough yet.

The *Triangular Powers* can be programmed to work against holiness because worldliness is a default. So, if a person is not choosing to walk in holiness, they will automatically do whatever the world is doing.

Parents, if your child is reading or showing interest in any kind of books on how to use the *magic* in the sun, or the moon or the stars, this is serious. You're responsible to teach your children at all times. Teach them right from wrong.

So if you were indoctrinated yourself by any of these *Triangular Powers* working against you, there are prayers of deliverance at the end of this book.

# 93 Million Miles Away

There's the sun. 93 million miles away. But we can still feel the effects of it because it's very powerful. It's huge, really. The sun is huge. It is aggressive, it's merciless. Ask anybody who lives in a desert type setting or lives in an arid environment like that. Someone told me that they've endured triple digit temperatures all last summer.

Wherever you are, the sun will *find* you.

The sun is relentless, and in my opinion, of all the *Triangular Powers*, the sun is boss, the sun is stronger, it's bigger, and all the other heavenly powers really depend on it.

The Earth rotates and orbits around the sun, and you know what you rotate around you are kind of tempted to worship it, but we **do not worship the sun**.

The last time you checked out a good-looking person, when you sized them up, didn't you *rotate* all around them?

It takes the Earth a year to fully go around the sun just one time. Because the sun is 864,000 miles in diameter, and it is 100 times larger than the Earth. The sun can make up 100 Earths in size and it is 10,000 degrees Fahrenheit on the surface.

**It's a star, it's a mega star, and it is the boss.**

# The Villain

Those who work evil have figured out or have been taught how to use the sun for wickedness. They're very determined and they are very **proud** of their "powers." They're proud of their ability to harness even a part of the power of the sun in an evil way.

Like the arch enemies of superhero movies, they are proud and arrogant enough to tell you **what they're going to do to you.** They will tell you nearly play by play how they are going to hurt you, or even destroy you. False bravado? No, they are sure of the power and ability that they can muster against an enemy.

My friends, listen, this is not a war on words on the part of the wizard or the evil person, the evil Enchanter, who's speaking to you, who's telling you what they're going to do to you. This is not child's play, it's not a child's war on a grade school playground.

If a person is telling you who they are, you need to believe them. If they tell you that they're about to do some *stuff* to you, you need to believe it. You don't need to talk back to them. You don't even need to engage your mouth against them. But by the Spirit of God, you have to not let it invoke fear in you. Fear will make their efforts all the more effective against you because fear is INSIDE you are wreaking havoc, causing the release of survival hormones that can make you hyper, bring your immune system down among other ill-effects.

You need to quickly abide in a place under the shadow of the Most High. You need to find a place of safety, but you need to get into spiritual warfare, quick, fast, and in a hurry.

People of God I admonish you, the person who's threatening you know their craft, they know their instruments, they know their weapons. They've practiced and they've been using them with great degrees of satisfaction, else they wouldn't be so confident.

Then said David to the Philistine, Thou comest to me with a sword, and with a spear, and with a shield: but I come to thee in the name of the LORD of hosts, the God of the armies of Israel, whom thou hast defied.

1 Samuel 17:45

When you know what is coming against you, you will know how to defend yourself. Exactly *who* is coming against you may not be known, unless they boldly tell you that it's them, or the Lord reveals to you who is coming against you. Your prayers may be general *whosoever* prayers. You may not know how or when, but God does; stay prayed up.

Know your own weapons that you will be using against this kind of evil, especially when it's in your face telling you what it's planning to do to you.

# Declared War

Christian saints of God, especially those who've been in church for 10, 20, or 30 years and each Sunday you've sung two hymns and listened to a 10-minute homily--, but you've done nothing else the rest of the week--, I'm talking to you right now. I'm admonishing you: The person who's threatening you knows their craft, they know their instruments, they know their weapons and they have been using them with evil success.

Now, I'm talking to the other Christians who go to the *fun* churches where the music is *crunk* and everybody's having fun and laughing at the entertaining preacher. And you, like the boring Christian, don't do anything else the rest of the week. I'm talking to you. Those people can't wait to get to church again on Sunday to have a good time, as if it's a club.

I'm talking to you. I admonish you: Do either of you two groups of Christians even know what your weapons of war are?

**A person really has just declared war--**, a spiritual war on you. Do you know what your weapons of war are? Do you know where they are, how to access them, how to get them, how to work them? Have you *ever* worked them? Yeah, prayer is one of your weapons.

Good, you know a whole 5-minute prayer, a thank-You-Jesus prayer. Well, that's good if you're thanking Jesus, right then. That's great if you're thanking Jesus, the one who just gave you 5-minutes' worth of blessings. For $5 you get $5 worth of gas in your car. So how much blessing, protection, love, Mercy or Grace does a 5-minute prayer get you?

Thanksgiving is necessary, but right now, with war declared, we need warfare.

**For every evil under the sun,**

 **there is a remedy.**

You have to know what your weapons are and how to work them, this is not child's play.

**There's a remedy or there's none. If there be one, try and find it. If there be none, never mind it.**

Well, there is one. You better find it, and you need to find it *before* you need it. You need to know how to work it and have had success with it *before* you actually need it, and especially at this level. This is the level where the declared enemy is *triangulating* with the sun against his enemies, and he's declared you an enemy.

There is a remedy, and the remedy in this case is spiritual warfare.

Oh, do you just have a plan to get somebody to do it for you? ***Well who?***

The pastor? Your praying friend--, or the pastor? Which one? Depends. Is the pastor even going to answer the phone in the middle of the night when you feel like something's not going *quite right*? Is your praying friend gonna get the phone at 2:00 AM when you think something's going sideways or you are seeing things in your house and fear and stress are rising within you? So, it might depend on which one of them answers the phone in your dire hour.

What if neither one of them takes your call?

<u>You</u> are supposed to know your weapons and how they work. **You** are supposed to be well-versed in spiritual warfare. You are supposed to be able to

withstand spiritual attacks. You should not be overrun by demons. Further, if need be, you need to be able to launch an offensive attack for your life, for your godliness, for your safety, for preservation of yourself and your family.

Then there's the *It Don't Take All That* crowd. Where are you? It **does** take all that and that what I just described is the *remedy* to this threat.

There was a pastor just this week who was threatened by a black magic agent, and the pastor went into a shouting match against her, challenging her to *bring it on.*

Really?

No, this is not the time for a rapper's beef. I didn't know that pastors did this public "beef" thing. This is not entertainment. This ain't that.

Know that a lot of the music industry *beefs* are fabricated for publicity. I know someone who works in that industry, who told me years ago most of the rappers are best friends.

We can go over to the professional boxers too while we're at it. Just like the staged wrestling we used to watch on TV.

Sorry folks hope I'm not ruining your fun. These celebrity *beefs* from any industry are staged to sell tickets, sell CD's and downloads. Come on.

You have to get prepared. You can't let your spiritual battles look like Will Smith slapped Chris Rock, and Chris Rock just stood there stunned. You can't be Chris Rock. Maybe you should be the slapper or the Holy Ghost slapper. Don't be the *slappee*; Christian, stop standing there stunned.

# Take Authority

You need to command the night, command the day, command these *Triangular Powers*. You need to be proactive, progressive, and you need to know someone if they're programming celestial bodies to your hurt or harm. You need to know what to do about it. You need to know you have authority to do something about it and then **do** something about it. Consider that evil programming into the celestial bodies most likely means that every night, every day, every noontime, cyclically with the rising and setting of these heavenly bodies what has been programmed will automatically happen to you.

Better stay prayed up.

Don't wait until the *slap* has already happened.

Witchcraft attacks are sudden, like out of the blue. If the villain *hasn't* announced it to you, it's unexpected. If the villain, evil human agent **has** announced it, it's still a surprise because who knows what they actually will do and really you don't know WHAT response it will elicit.

The attack could actually be subtle--, doesn't have to be, but it can be. You know something is off, but you're not really sure *what, or* where.

In ***Upgrade: How to Get Out of Survival Mode*** Series, *Book 1,* I talk a lot about the signs of witchcraft attack, you need to check those out. They will teach you a lot.

There are witches, warlocks, wizards, some enchanters that have been born into that lifestyle. I'm not celebrating them; I just want you aware that some have this stuff in their bloodline. It's generational and they've been doing it a long time.

You'd better know.

So there you are having been saved for *years* but you've never done anything but just float along, thinking the pastor is going to do everything, suddenly this level of attack comes upon you. Really, are you going to counter the attack?

**Unopposed, witchcraft is powerful.** It is a real thing.

There's a remedy, and the greater one is in us. Amen. The greater one is in us, and that is the remedy.

These enchanters are working with *familiar spirits* that have already sized you up. They know *if* you don't know what you're doing. They do. They've already sized you up and they know that if they attack you if you will be an easy target or not.

But God!

Any of us could be an easy target for any level of black arts, but for our God! But the greater one is in us.

So if these evil spirits, or these evil human agents, the enchanters are checking for you and they find that you're in God, Spirit-filled, a workman who studies to show yourself approved they will rethink their strategy. If they find that you're a prayer warrior, or you're not slack in the things of God, they might just keep on stepping by you. They're not gonna bother you because you also have a hedge of protection around you. Thank God by the Blood of Jesus, by the fire of the Holy Spirit, and that hedge could be so strong, that wall could be so strong that they couldn't penetrate if they tried.

The greater one is in us.

The Name of the Lord is a strong tower. The righteous Run in it. They're safe. Hallelujah.

Every dark arrow fired at me, fire back, in the Name of Jesus.

# Sun Power

Witchcraft programmed with the *Triangular Powers* of the sun, the moon, and/or the stars can make a person feel like they're another whole man all of a sudden, and maybe not in a good way.

It's like the brain gets hijacked. This is all part of witchcraft attack. When (if) you finally come back to your senses, you might wonder what in the world happened to you.

There's evil under the sun. For every evil under the sun, there's a remedy.

If you're not working the *remedy*, then there is none.

If you're waiting for someone else to work the remedy for you and they can't come to your assistance, there is no remedy.

# Household Enemies

Matthew 10:36 tells us that the enemies of a man are the members of his own household. Household enemies use your secrets to their own advantage. First thing, like a stranger with the *familiar spirit,* they're gonna size you up.

Will you be an easy target, or will you give you give them trouble or an impossibility in their plans?

Let your plan be to fight spiritually. Please!

Household witchcraft which usually stems from jealousy and resentment is to old enemies goal is to bring you down a notch or two. This enemy is pretending to be your friend, or maybe this person *is* your relative, but they really don't want to be your friend.

I'm not trying to pit families against each other, but you need your eyes open. You need to be wise. So do I. We need to pray and pray and pray.

It may be that the antagonists in our family, maybe they will get saved one day for real, and stop doing this stuff and dabbling in the witchcraft. But in the meantime, you have to protect yourself and your family, your career, your life, your purpose, your ministry. You need to protect your life--, protect everything.

But you're saying it's my family. How am I going to get away from them? You can't really. Maybe you can for a while during the year, but Mom or Dad or somebody wants you to come home for Christmas, for Mother's Day, for Easter, for Father's Day, for Thanksgiving. There you all are, sitting at the table again, having a meal together.

You are renewing your family covenants. You know, the ones you got away from all year you've been praying against. You're renewing your family dynamics, renewing your bloodline altars--, now familial and generational *stuff* can continue to keep happening to you.

Anyone who is uncomfortable with my promotion, I forbid your hatred to come to me in the Name of Jesus.

Anyone uncomfortable with my new position, lose your position, in the Name of Jesus.

Anyone uncomfortable with my success or my relationship with God, may the Lord find you and change your heart, in the Name of Jesus.

You do realize that in a house, in a family, and a workplace there are people competing with you. You may have no idea that they're competing with you because you're not a competitive person. Therefore, you are not competing against them.

Some of these people are in your own family. Now that I mention it--, *IKR?*

But God is good to us. We are on assignment in the Earth, and God is supplying all of our needs according to His riches in glory. God gives us what we need.

Where's the stuff? What's the holdup? We talked about this in the **Powers Above** book. Once your prayers, your things and your blessings and your prayers going both directions pass through the heavenlies, you should get your answers and responses without delay. Daniel 10:12-13. But there's a war out there. There's a war zone. In that war zone, in the heavenlies are the principalities, powers and spiritual wickedness in high places working with evil human agents, using *Triangular Powers* to interfere with your success, life, accomplishments, education, ministry, marriage, family – any and all of that!

# SUNBLOCK

There are heavenly powers that are programmed against you to hold up your blessings and to interfere with your relationship with God. So we have to be doing something spiritually while all this is happening, and we need to at least be defensive and put on some sunblock. Not the kind we smear on our skin at the beach, but we need some *spiritual* sunblock.

We need the powers of God and the weapons of God to help us, the Blood of Jesus, the angels, the warring angels of God, and the power and the fire of the Holy Ghost to block the things that the sun may be programmed to do against us, in the Name of Jesus. So God has warrior angels because warrior angels are involved in warfare.

To strike, damage or afflict with heavy blows. Witchcraft attack is usually not a one-off. Those sending evil arrows mean it and they want to afflict for sure and worse, most of the time. God is your only help; stay prayed up. Be instant in payer. Pray without ceasing. Be wise to the enemy's tactics. Even if attacks are coming at you block them, if they are heavy blows, coming at you nearly relentlessly, triangulated with the sun, SUNBLOCK them with warfare prayer.

Familiar spirits advise these evil human agents of the best time to attack you. It is sobering to think people can read your temperature in the Spirit. If an evil man can, surely God knows all this about you. The more prayerful you are the more fired up you are the hotter you are in the Spirit. When you are very hot, the enemies of God will go right past you.

Lord, make me fire so that I am too hot for my enemies, in the Name of Jesus.

The *Powers Above*, when used against mankind, very effective against people who don't believe there's anything going on. That bored, crunk, unstudied, untaught Christian is not going to fight.

You're not one of those people. Amen.

You **will** fight. You will possess your possessions. You are not one of those people who has a form of godliness and denies the power of it.

We are supposed to forgive fellow Christians. The Word says forgive people for their slights, but when people are out to destroy you, and are enchanting against you--, that calls for the whole armor. That calls for spiritual warfare, and it calls for warfare prayer--, it calls for *spiritual* sunblock.

# While the Sun Slept

Evil is not stronger than good, but can it be that evil dedication is stronger than Christian dedication? Enchanters are up all night, enchanting, chanting, muttering spells and enchantments against their would-be victims.

They are even programming the sun--, the sun is still asleep, and they're programming the sun. Christians, where are we? Oh, we're asleep, most of the time, and by the time we wake up, the evil is already spoken, it's already set. It's already established.

Christians, their unsuspecting victims, where were you again? Oh, you were asleep, thinking that Christianity is just a passive thing, you get saved and then it's something you do on Sunday. No, it's way more than that. So you've put yourself on the bench, as it were, in this game. You've put *yourself* there. God didn't put you there; He didn't say go live your life, doing whatever you think is right, until you die.

And look, it's not even a bench that you're on. You bought a lazy boy recliner onto the battlefield, and it's a whole war. This is not that!

I'm calling you action. Yes, I'm calling you to prayer and to practice the disciplines of Christianity.

I'm telling you, there are over 1,000,000 practicing the black arts in the USA alone right now.

There is a remedy for us because Jesus came to Earth. Jesus came to give us power and authority over this evil, and we must use it. The Greater One is in us. Amen.

We should not ever appear to be defeated, else what will our Christian witness look like if we look beat down, busted and disgusted every week?

# They Should Be Very Afraid

***Why are we even being attacked?*** Shouldn't we as Christians shouldn't be enchanters be ***afraid*** of us because of our God? Yeah, if we're doing something, they should be afraid of us. But they're not if they're unopposed, because they're powerful unopposed. They're not if we're not doing anything. They're not scared of us if we are in our lazy boy, asleep. We should have a Sword of the Spirit in our hands, not the TV remote.

There are some people even alleged Christians, who may want enchantments done against you. They will go and *pay* someone to do things against you. You've got to be prayerful and discerning. Every friend is not a friend.

This is real. It's not the same for us--, it's not as though Christians could pay somebody to defend us so we can *sleep*.

People who want evil done against proclaimed enemies do go and pay people to enchant against their would-be victims. They'd even pay multiple people. A whole coven will take the job and they will enchant all night while the one who paid the money is asleep. Do not think that a witchcraft attack against you is one solitary witch--, that might not be the case at all.

You'd better stay prayed up.

# See To It Yourself

We talked about pastors and so-called pastors' in **Powers Above: Triangular Powers**. Again I tell you that you will have to do your own warfare, *yourself*. Even if you have a good pastor, he might be praying for you. He or she may be praying for you, but they're not praying *instead* of you. See to it yourself, do it yourself.

The fact that a witchcraft attack *hit* is enough information for you to know that you're not covered in Teflon, you're not wearing spiritual Kevlar; you are not *covered* like you think. Yes, you're saved. Getting saved is the authority to do the spiritual things you need to do. It is not a spiritual all-inclusive vacay where you do nothing but enjoy yourself from here on out. Getting saved is not a spiritual retirement home where you also do nothing until Glory.

Awake from your slumber. **See to it yourself**. Prayer is not just for your own spiritual protection. It's for the whole body of Christ. You pray and go into warfare because you're in covenant with God, God's enemies are your enemies, your enemies are His.

God's fighting for you. What are you doing?

You want God to fight *instead* of you? If God tells you to stand down, then stand down, else continue to fight *spiritually* in prayer, praise and worship.

Yeah, God is able. He's strong, He's mighty, He's powerful, He's an all-consuming God. But you're assigned to Earth right now and set in Dominion—for a reason.

Let me go into that a little bit. Heaven and Earth must agree. Some things cannot even happen in the Earth until we **agree** with God. Until we agree with the 3rd Heaven.

There the Enchanters are, up all night, agreeing with the 2nd heaven so evil can come to Earth. They are summonsing up evil from the pit of Hell. They're doing it all day. They have altars.

Do you have an altar?

They may be up all night, or they get up at midnight, which is the witching hour. From midnight to 6:00 AM is a very dangerous time for Christians because we're **asleep**. The Enchanters are up enchanting.

Then there's the 3rd Heaven, where God dwells, where God lives, and God needs the people of God to make **agreement** in the Earth so things from the 3rd Heaven can happen here on the Earth.

# Why Is It So Quiet At Your House, *at Night?*

I must ask you: Why is it so quiet at your house? *Oh---*, you're asleep. You should be praying, but you're asleep.

We need to put on the whole spiritual armor of God, because there's a battle--, there's a war. If you had any idea of the people who can't stand you right now, who hate you, just because you're a Christian, -- they don't even know you, but they are doing things against you because that's their assignment, and you're the target, the would-be victim.

Proclaim you this among the Gentiles.
Prepare war.
Wake up, the mighty men of war.
(Joel 3:9)

# Not A Quick Study

The spiritual war that is going on right now concerns you. The war that broke out in Heaven concerns you. The war in the warzone in the second heaven concerns you and the warfare of witchcraft attack that may have located you or your household deeply concerns you.

All of these battles and wars impact your life, your health, your peace, your business, your career, your education, your family, your marriage, your whole bloodline, your purpose, your provision, your wealth and welfare, your destiny and the devil is not a quick study, else we wouldn't still be getting tricked by him.

At my place of business, over many years, I've heard so many people who have applied for positions, and they love to tell me they're *quick learners*. That has been false 99 or more percent of the time. So my new stance is, *"You are a quick learner? Good. Go learn this and then come back with a certificate to prove to me that you've learned it."*

If a person can learn in 15 minutes or a week, something that takes two years for the average person to learn, how are they not a genius? A brain surgeon? A rocket scientist? Why do they NOT *have* a job already?

The Devil's like that--, he's not a quick study either. We can't learn all the devil's wiles and tricks at church one Sunday, we have to STUDY to show ourselves approved. We have to study him; go learn. Be as a workman: Study to rightly divide the Word of God. Actually learn some Word so we can use it and rightly divide it, so we are not embarrassed, ashamed, afflicted or defeated when attacks may come our way. Even when strong attacks that have been triangulated with the sun come our way.

Nowhere in the Bible does it say here are some weapons, but you don't need to know about that.

Nowhere in the Bible does it say, here's some armor, some spiritual armor, but that doesn't apply to you. Put it in a chest over there and put a lock on it. No, it doesn't say that.

Nowhere in the Bible does it say, here's a Bible, but you don't have to read it. We'll just give you the few verses on the program on Sunday. You don't have to read your Bible. No, Real Christians read their own Bible. It is their manual for living. It's their manual of warfare when warfare is needed.

Christian dedication shows. Are you *dedicated* to being a Christian? Doing what Christians do, or are you just dedicated to knowing a few words and facts, that you can talk about with your friends?

Resist the devil and he'll flee from you.
(James 4:7)

Nowhere in the Bible does it say to ignore the devil.

Nowhere in the Bible does it say to pretend that that the devil doesn't exist. Nowhere.

God is waiting for us to **agree** with Heaven. *Let it be done on Earth as it is in Heaven.*

We don't worship angels, but when we pray the mighty Angels of God come for our words, (Daniel 10:12). If it's a crisis and the Lord gets out of it, then we need to keep praying, keep praying, keep praying. Praying once --it's your 5-minute prayer, it's not enough.

**It shouldn't be so quiet at your house.**

Your TV is agreeing with the 2nd heaven. Turn it off and you agree with the 3rd Heaven where God lives. The world agrees with the 2nd Heaven; you have to pray. God has plans for your future and your life and a good result for your life and destiny.

God has answered your prayers. If it seems like He has not, it could be that *Triangular Powers* have been enchanted against you to hold you back, to stagnate you, to turn you, to make you take one step forward and two steps back.

The world even sings songs that celebrate the stuff that evil does to people. Don't you also sing it else you'll be agreeing with the 2nd heaven. Again.

# Agree With God

Instead, agree with God. Agree with the Word of God and what it says in the Bible. Agree with the 3rd Heaven. There's nothing more important on TV than your real life. You need prayers answered. You may need healing. You need provisions. You need your blessings to locate you here on Earth.

All the while the enemy, the devil is trying to corrupt your communication and your *relationship* with God, break up your provision and blessings network from God that allows what He sends to actually get to you.

The thrust of all of this is to drive you into unbelief, disappointment, trauma, and desperation which the devil hopes will lead you into idolatry. In idolatry a desperate person may take matters "into their own hands" and seek ungodly, unorthodox measures to meet his needs, or desires. This may take a person straight into the hands or jaws, of the devil because the devil would love to devour any Christian.

No! Agree with the 3rd Heaven. Instead, *Let it be done on Earth as it is in Heaven.* Make Earth look like Heaven.

You want Jesus to return? I think if we made the place a bit more inviting, we might encourage Him to come back.

We need to put on our whole armor every day because *a war*, (Revelations 12:7), broke out in Heaven.

Frustrated, you may be saying, *Oh well, I pray, but nothing happened.* Then keep praying! You didn't get into this mess into this pickle in one day. So we can't expect it to be cleared up in an hour, in a day, or in your 5-minute prayer.

The *Powers Above*, especially the sun, wields a lot of power. Those who know how to work it for evil are working it. We Christians need to know how to work it. God made it for **us**, not for them. Those who know how to work it for good--, we need to be those people who know how to work it for good. We need to cry out to God because He made all of creation to serve us.

# A Time for War

We are set in Dominion with authority, and we need to *work it*. We need to work it, we need to work that authority, and then we need to pray.

Build up your spiritual warfare and your spiritual weapons so you will be prepared at the onslaught of the enemy.

Remember, there is a remedy for every evil under the sun, there's a remedy. Even if evil is triangulated with the sun, there is sunblock, and that sunblock is spiritual warfare. The Greater One is in us. Amen.

We need to be working the *Powers Above*, if not, someone could be doing the opposite against us.

Yes, we're even supposed to be doing good to people who hate us. That's what the Bible says. But, what if someone is out to kill you, to end your life, and destroy your entire bloodline? --Let me interrupt now and ask when is it a ***time of war***, as in Ecclesiastes 3?

A time to love, and a time to hate; a time of war, and a time of peace. (Ecclesiastes 3:8)

Wartime not forgiveness time. That's back to sender time. That's spiritual warfare time.

Suffer not a witch to live. We wrestle not against flesh and blood, but against spiritual wickedness. Witchcraft is spiritual wickedness. Return to sender is NOT a death decree or prayer against the witch, it is against the witchcraft. To what degree a person has embraced the witchcraft and *become* the witchcraft is between that person and God.

To what degree a person has become a Christian and become a Son of God is judged by God.

God does as He will with humans in the Earth; He knows who will be saved and who will not ever repent. That is between God and that person. Return to sender is to devastate the *witchcraft*, the power that is causing destruction and havoc in one's life, it is not a judgment or sentence on the human that is attached to the witchcraft.

In our own sin God allows us to put an end to sin without killing us; He is merciful. God is also a God of Vengeance. If sinners, seekers and even Christians continue in sin, God is the Righteous Judge.

Sin is sin.

Witchcraft is sin.

For every evil under the sun, there is a remedy. Amen.

Arise, mighty warrior, get out of your lazy boy chair. Get out of your rocking chair. Put on the whole armor of God. Put on the whole armor of light. It's time to do some warfare to assist our angels and their works on our behalf in the Earth.

We are responsible for praying all types of prayer. In every season in Ecclesiastes and in our lives we pray appropriately to our Father, God. Those inclined to warfare have to temper warfare with other prayers when indicated. Those who like the sweet, loving prayers must learn warfare prayers. Different seasons of our lives require different prayer types.

There are Mary's and there are Martha's. We all are who we are in God and to God. This book is about sunblock, that is blocking the effects of the triangulation of Triangular Powers to cause devastation in the life of a would-be witchcraft victim. The sunblock, as I have said, is spiritual warfare.

Let's get to it.

# Wake Me Up WARFARE

Father, in the Name of Jesus, wake me up. Get me up when it's time to pray.

Fill me up with the power of God and the Holy Spirit. Fill me with the *Spirit of prayer* so that I pray all kinds of prayers, and I am effective in the Spirit, in the Name of Jesus.

Lord, if anyone is enchanting against me, **wake me up.**

Wake me up if I'm sleeping.

Get me up. If I'm resting.

Stir me up if I'm idle.

And Fire me up by the Holy Spirit, in the Name of Jesus.

Lord, Arise and contend with those who contend with me. Thank you, Lord, in the Name of Jesus

Every power swallowing my powers and my prayers, I command your stomach to burst into flames and vomit my powers and prayers, in the Name of Jesus.

Enemies of the Most High God, I deafen your ears. I am speaking to my Father, not to you now, in the Name of Jesus. I take authority over the effects of the elements, especially the *Triangular Powers*, the sun, the moon and the stars, by commanding the day and also commanding the night, in the Name of Jesus.

Every Angel of God working on my behalf or on the behalf of God and what's good. Be strengthened, mighty angels be encouraged, be forceful, be mighty and strong, be victorious, and finish every task to the glory of God. Amen.

I command the Earth to receive heavenly instructions on my behalf. I command all the elements of Creation to take heed and obey as I praise, as my praise resounds, and the dawn breaks, Lord let the Earth yield Her increase to me.

I prophesy the will of God to the morning, so that the first light shall shake wickedness from the four corners of the Earth.

Every dark power using *Triangular Powers* to attack me, die, in the Name of Jesus.

Lord, disconnect my life from all evil using *Triangular Powers* against me, in the Name of Jesus.

Every evil arrow from the sun, moon, and stars, release me; back to your sender, in the Name of Jesus.

Every enchanter, witch, wizard, any agent of darkness working against me, either on your own behalf or by proxy, forget my name, lose my location, in the Name of Jesus.

Heavens refuse to conduct warfare against my life, in the Name of Jesus.

Anything that is blocking the heavenlies from fighting for me, come out, come up, come out, come up and out, in the Name of Jesus.

Lord, I receive deliverance now, in the mighty Name of Jesus Christ.

All evil programmed into my bloodline from the sun, be cancelled right now, in the Name of Jesus.

Sun, reject every evil incantation, hex, vex, spell, or enchantment intended for me. I fire back to sender, in the Name of Jesus.

Blood of Jesus, wipe away all evil handwriting that is in the sun, moon, stars or anywhere in the heavenlies against me, in the Name of Jesus.

I command the *Triangular Powers*, the *Powers Above* to fight for me, not against me, in the Name of Jesus.

Sun, you were created by God, and you should have obey the Voice of the Word of God. Do not smite me by day, not this day or any day, in the Name of Jesus.

Moon, you were created by God, and you must obey the Voice of the Word of

God. Do not smite me by night, not this night or any night, in the Name of Jesus.

Stars and every element in the skies and heavens, you were created by God, and you should obey the Voice of the Word of God. Do not smite me by day or by night, not this or any day or night, in the Name of Jesus.

Lord, raise an opponent against the enemies of my life and my destiny, in the Name of Jesus.

Lord, I release heavy fog, dense smoke, Fire and confusion into the camp of my enemies, in the Name of Jesus.

In the Name of Jesus, Lord cause memory loss to my enemies that they forget how to enchant against me and they lose my coordinates, location and position at all times.

Break every network with monitoring and familiar spirits of those who seek after my hurt, harm, loss or destruction in the Name of Jesus.

Angels of God, chase every demon that threatens my life back to the abyss from where there is no return, in the Name of Jesus.

Every evil person, entity, or power that is working against my life, my health, my success, my marriage, my family, Lord Jesus cut off their power from the powers of all the elements, in the Name of Jesus.

Lord cut off their power from the powers of the sun, moon, and stars, in the Name of Jesus.

Lord, shut off their evil powers from the water, seas, oceans, rivers, any water, in the Name of Jesus.

Lord, disconnect the powers of all evil human agents working against me from the Earth, the soil, stones, mountains, and trees, in the Name of Jesus.

Lord, disconnect their powers from the network of other *witchcraft spirits* by the power of Fire, in the Name of Jesus.

Lord, stop their powers from the wind, the sky, and any fire, in the Name of Jesus.

Father, stop all *Triangular Powers* from working against me, in the Name of Jesus.

By Thunder by fire I break up every altar erected against me, in the Name of Jesus. (X3)

Any evil altar automatically emanating curses against me, catch fire and roast to ashes now, in the Name of Jesus.

Any evil persecutor of any description, the Lord smite you with fear and confusion that you turn back from your assignment against me, in the Name of Jesus.

Every evil incantation uttered into the sun, moon, stars, water, Earth, wind, fire, stone, any pot or plate charm anything against me. Be nullified by the Blood of Jesus. (X3)

Every witchcraft kitchen cooking up evil food for me catch fire and burn all the way down, in the Name of Jesus.

Any power working against me, fall into the abyss from where you cannot return, in the Name of Jesus.

Every altar against me, programmed into the sun, moon, or stars, lose your programming, lose your calendar, lose your clock and timer against me and roast to ashes by fire and brimstone. Right now, in the Name of Jesus,

Fire of God, I call down fire. I call down fire. I call down fire against every evil altar erected or working against me or my bloodline, in the Name of Jesus.

Fire, Fire, Fire, I call down fire of God, put a hedge of Fire around me, a wall of Fire Lord, a mountain of Fire and make me too hot for my enemies to even come close, in the name of Jesus.

My life, be charged with Fire of God and no evil and no demon can touch it, in the Name of Jesus.

Charms that get their strength from any or all of the *Triangular Powers*, I command you to lose all potency against me, in the Name of Jesus; return to sender.

Any enchantment of any satanic entity or human agent, backfire by Fire, in the Name of Jesus.

Every evil program to do with the sun against my relationships, against my family life, the Lord Jesus block all access to me. Whatever you have planned for me, let it happen to you, in the Name of Jesus.

Every arrow from the sun, moon and stars. Release me and locate your owner back to sender, in the Name of Jesus. *Triangular Powers* go to war **for** me, not against me, in the Name of Jesus.

Every evil human agent, now is Salvation, may the Lord find you and locate your heart and turn it from evil to good, in the Name of Jesus.

All unrepentant agents of evil, I commend you to the feet of Jesus Christ for ministry, in the Name of Jesus.

Every evil that is followed by parents stop following me. I belong to Christ, in the name of Jesus.

I command the night and the day.

I command the sun, and the moon, and the stars that you will not smite me, but you'll work in my favor for my goodness, for my success, for my blessings, prosperity, business, life, relationships, in the Name of Jesus.

Thank You, Lord. I count as done, in the mighty Name of Jesus.

Jesus, I invite you into my life, into my household, to expose every household enemy, all wickedness, in the Name of Jesus.

Thank You, Lord, for the Wisdom, the authority, and the power to deal with it all, in the Name of Jesus. Thank You, Lord.

Thank you, Lord.

**Amen.**

## Dear Reader

Thank you for acquiring, reading, and sharing this book. I pray that it will make you wiser and better equipped to deal with what may come up against you. Better than that, may you preempt the strikes the enemy has planned against you by being *prayed up.*

God bless you,

In the Name of Jesus,

**Amen.**

Dr. Marlene Miles

# Prayer books by this author

While most books by this author have prayer points either throughout the book or at the end, there are some books that are **only** prayers. You just open up the book and pray. They are listed below:

**Prayers Against Barrenness:** *For Success in Business and Life*

**Fruit of the Womb:** *Prayers Against Barrenness*

**Beauty Curses,** *Warfare Prayers Against*
https://a.co/d/5Xlc20M

**Courts of Marriage: Prayers for Marriage in the Courts of Heaven** *(prayerbook)*
https://a.co/d/cNAdgAq

## Courtroom Warfare @ Midnight
*(prayerbook)* https://a.co/d/5fc7Qdp

## Demonic Cobwebs *(prayerbook)*
https://a.co/d/fp9Oa2H

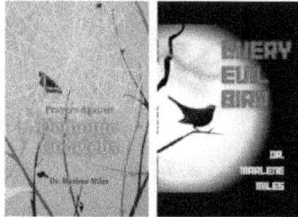

## Every Evil Bird https://a.co/d/hF1kh1O

## Every Evil Arrow https://a.co/d/afgRkiA

## Gates of Thanksgiving

## Spirits of Death & the Grave, Pass Over Me and My House https://a.co/d/dS4ewyr

*\*Please note that my name is spelled incorrectly on amazon, but not on the book.*

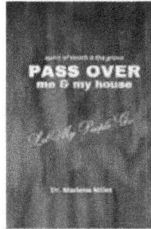

## Throne of Grace: Courtroom Prayer

https://a.co/d/fNMxcM9

## Warfare Prayer Against Poverty
https://a.co/d/bZ611Yu

## Other books by this author
**Abundance of Jesus,** *The*

**AK:** *The Adventures of the Agape Kid*

**AMONG SOME THIEVES**

**Ancestral Powers** https://a.co/d/9prTyFf

**Backstabbers** https://a.co/d/gi8iBxf

**Barrenness,** *Prayers Against*
https://a.co/d/feUltIs

**Battlefield of Marriage,** *The*

**Beware of the Dog:** *Prayers Against Dogs in the Dream*

**Blindsided:** *Has the Old Man Bewitched You?* https://a.co/d/5O2fLLR

**Break Free from Collective Captivity**

Caged Life https://a.co/d/0eKxbU9H

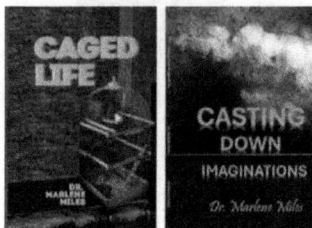

Casting Down Imaginations
https://a.co/d/1UxlLqa

Churchcraft: Witchcraft In the Church

Churchzilla, The Wanna-Be, Supposed-to-be Bride of Christ

Curses of Blind Men

Demonic Cobwebs (prayerbook)

Demonic Time Bombs

Demons Hate Questions (mini book)

Devil Loves Trauma, *The*

Devil Weapons: Unforgiveness, Bitterness,…

The Devourers: *Thieves of Darkness 2*

Do Not Swear by the Moon

Don't Refuse Me, Lord (4 book series)

https://a.co/d/idP34LG

Dream Defilement

The Emptiers: *Thieves of Darkness, 1*
https://a.co/d/5I4n5mc

Every Evil Arrow https://a.co/d/afgRkiA

Evil Touch https://a.co/d/gSGGpS1

Failed Assignment https://a.co/d/3CXtjZY

Fantasy Spirit Spouse
https://a.co/d/hW7oYbX

FAT Demons (The): *Breaking Demonic Curses*

The Fold (5-book series)

- The Fold (Book 1)
- Name Your Seed (Book 2)
- The Poor Attitudes of Money (3)
- Do Not Orphan Your Seed (4)
- For the Sake of the Gospel (5)
- My Sowing Journal

Gang Ups: *Touch Not God's Anointed*

got HEALING? Verses for Life

got LOVE? Verses for Life

got HOPE? Verses for Life

got money? https://a.co/d/g2av41N

Has My Soul Been Sold?

How to Dental Assist

How to Dental Assist2: Be Productive, Not Wasteful

I Take It Back

Legacy

Let Me Have A Dollar's Worth
https://a.co/d/h8F8XgE

Level the Playing Field
https://www.youtube.com/watch?v=BfF-TX1EWNQ

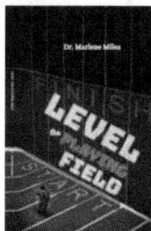

Living for the NOW of God

Lose My Location https://a.co/d/crD6mV9

Love Breaks Your Heart

Man Safari, *The* (mini book from The Wilderness Romance)

Marriage Ed. Rules of Engagement & Marriage

Made Perfect in Love

Money Hunters: Beware of Those

Money on the Altar https://a.co/d/4EqJ2Nr

Mulberry Tree https://a.co/d/9nR9rRb

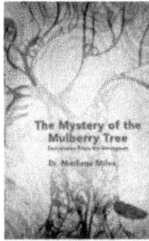

Motherboard (The) - *Soul Prosperity Series*

Name Your Seed

Occupy: *Until I Return*

Plantation Souls

Players Gonna Play

Power Money: Nine Times the Tithe

https://a.co/d/gRt41gy

Powers Above

Repent of Visiting Evil Altars
https://a.co/d/3n3Zjwx

The Robe, *Part 1, The Lessons of Joseph*

The Robe, *The Lessons of Joseph* Part II,

Seasons of Grief

Seasons of Waiting

Seasons of War

Second Marriage, Third--, *Any Marriage*
https://a.co/d/6m6GN4N

Sift You Like Wheat

Six Men Short: What Has Happened to all the Men?

Son https://a.co/d/09mIThSg

Soul Prosperity, Soul Prosperity Series Bk 3
https://a.co/d/5p8YvCN

Souls Captivity, Soul Prosperity Series Book 2

The Spirit of Poverty

StarStruck

SUNBLOCK

The Swallowers: *Thieves of Darkness*, Book 3

Take It Back

This Is NOT That: How to Keep Demons from Coming at You

Time Is of the Essence

Too Many Wives: *Why You Have Lady Problems*

Tormenting Spirits   https://a.co/d/dAogEJf

Toxic Souls

Triangular Power *(series)*

- Powers Above
- SUNBLOCK
- Do Not Swear by the Moon
- STARSTRUCK

Unbreak My Heart: *Don't Let Me Die*
Uncontested Doom

Unguarded Hours, *The*

Unseen Life, *The* https://a.co/d/0drZ5Ll

Upgrade: How to Get Out of Survival Mode (and two more titles):

- Toxic Souls (Book 2 of series)
- Legacy (Book 3 of series)

WTH? Get Me Out of This Hell

**The Wasters:** *Thieves of Darkness,* Bk 2
https://a.co/d/bUvI9Jo

**What Have You to Declare? What Do You Have With You from Where You've Been?**

**When I Was A Child,** *I Prayed As a Child*

**When the Devourer is Rebuked**

https://a.co/d/1HVv8oq

**The Wilderness Romance *(series)*** This series is about conducting a Godly relationship and marriage with someone who is a Wilderness person. It is about how to recognize it and navigate through it. These books are about how not to get caught up in such.

- *The Social Wilderness*
- *The Sexual Wilderness*
- *The Spiritual Wilderness*

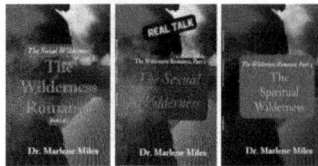

## Other Series
### Matters of the Heart series

Made Perfect in Love https://a.co/d/70MQW3O

Love Breaks Your Heart https://a.co/d/4KvuQLZ

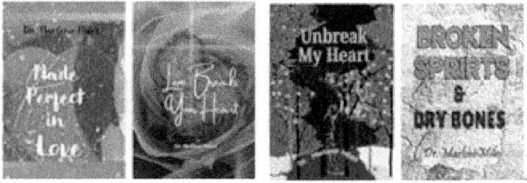

Unbreak My Heart https://a.co/d/84ceZ6M

Broken Spirits & Dry Bones
https://a.co/d/e6iedNP

The Fold (a series on Godly finances)
https://a.co/d/4hz3unj

Soul Prosperity Series https://a.co/d/bz2M42q

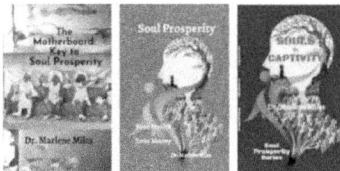

# Spirit Spouse books

https://a.co/d/9VehDSo

https://a.co/d/97sKOwm

**Thieves of Darkness** series

https://a.co/d/b07c8Ms

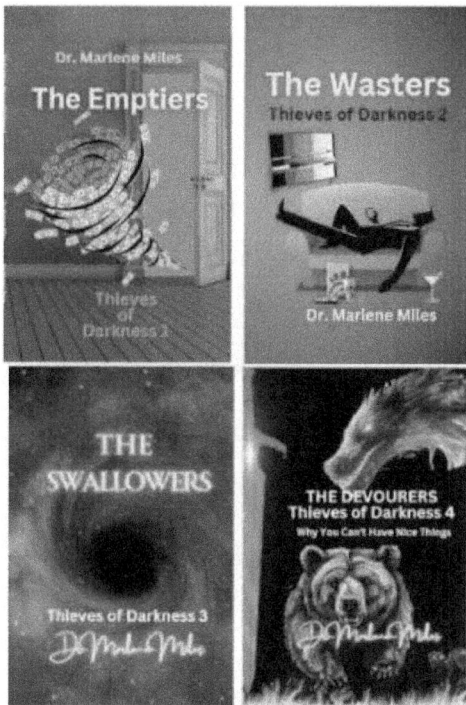

**Triangular Powers** https://a.co/d/aUCjAWC

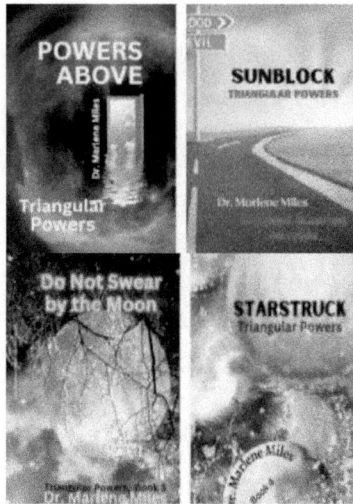

**Upgrade** (series) *How to Get Out of Survival Mode*
https://a.co/d/aTERhXO

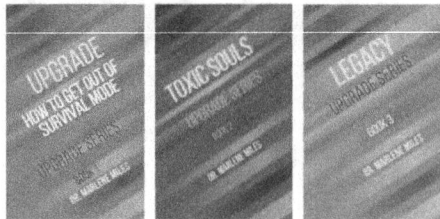

www.ingramcontent.com/pod-product-compliance
Lightning Source LLC
LaVergne TN
LVHW051424080426
835508LV00022B/3230